Dear Tiffany,

Happy 3rd Birthday! You are
such a smart, beautiful little
girl. + we love you.

Love,

Darrell, Jaca, Quincy + Nile

S0-ABC-621

To:

From:

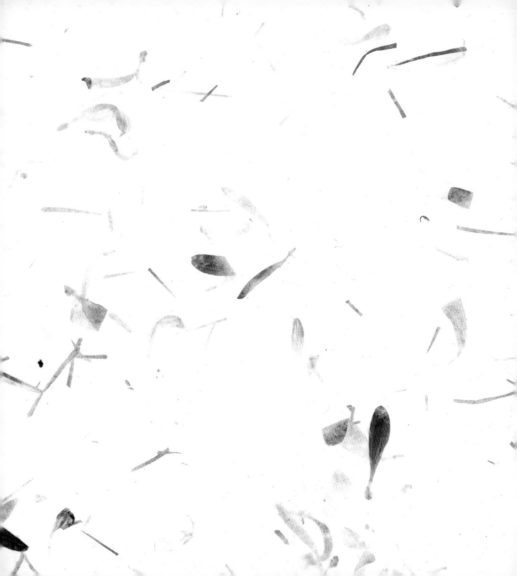

I Love You Beary Much

The Boyds Collection Ltd.®

Text written by Patrick Regan

**Andrews McMeel
Publishing**

Kansas City

I Love You Beary Much

Copyright © 2004 by The Boyds Collection Ltd.® All rights reserved. Printed in China.
No part of this book may be used or reproduced in any manner whatsoever without
written permission except in the case of reprints in the context of reviews.
For information, write Andrews McMeel Publishing, an Andrews McMeel Universal company,
4520 Main Street, Kansas City, Missouri 64111.

04 05 06 07 08 WKT 10 9 8 7 6 5 4 3 2 1

ISBN: 0-7407-4682-0

Library of Congress Control Number: 2004102688

Book design by Holly Camerlinck

I Love You
Beary Much

Psst . . . can you keep a secret?

I know I can trust you, so I'll let you in on a little something.

There's someone you know who
I've grown awfully fond of.

*You might even say I'm
head over heels.*

No . . . I won't tell you who it is

just yet,

But sit back, and I'll tell you a few things about this certain someone.

First of all, my secret love
is sweeter than honey

And realizes that love is shown
in lots of little ways.

My special someone
always seems to know
when I'm feeling a little down

And has been known to go to
great lengths to cheer me up!

with this person around,
I get my smile back before I know it.

Honestly, there are times when my secret crush is an absolute life preserver.

I love my sweetie more than
ice cream—and you know that's
saying something!

Haven't guessed who I'm talking about yet? Okay, I'll give you a few more clues.

*My sweetheart can be
a little shy sometimes*

But is always loads of fun!

The object of my affection
is also very smart

And is both interesting to listen to
and interested in what I have to say.

(And you don't meet too many folks like that anymore.)

Being with this amazing person
makes me feel like anything
is possible

And reminds me that when

we sow seeds of love,

*Bountiful blossoms are just
bound to bloom.*

Love is
meant to
be shared

I'm sure you know the type—
the kind of person you want to
share all your favorite things with.

And when they're not around,
life can feel a bit unbearable.

*I can always be myself with
this person—as comfortable as
a favorite pair of slippers.*

(Though sometimes we like to get dressed up for each other too!)

Oh, did I mention that my
secret sweetie is cute as a button?

(Yes, I'm biased, but it's true!)

And one more hint . . .
this person gives the absolute
best hugs in the world!

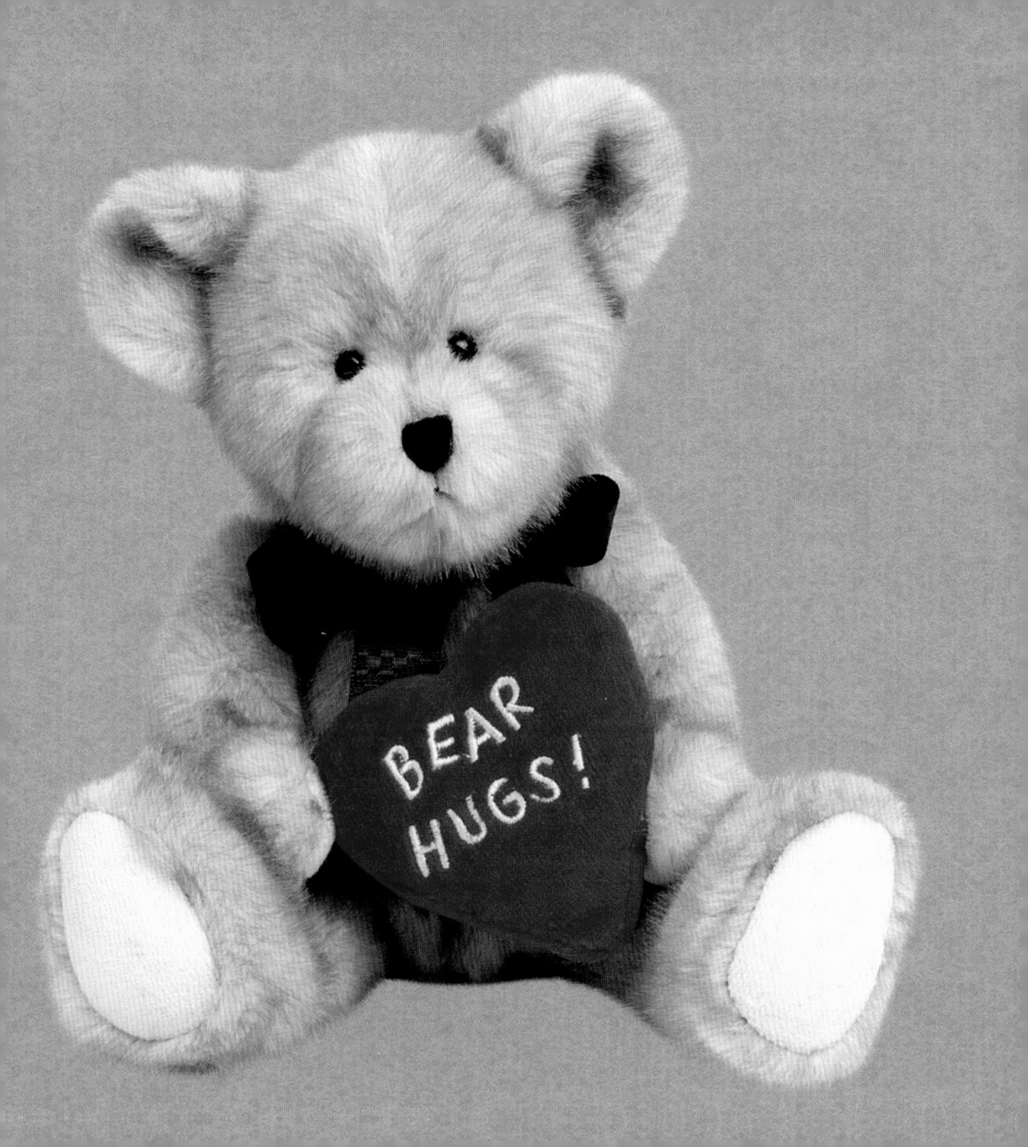
BEAR
HUGS!

*So, have you figured out
my secret yet?*

Come closer and I'll whisper it
in your ear.

It's you, silly bear!

You're the one who makes
my heart warm on cold days,

puts a spring in my step,

And brings a sparkle to my eyes.

You and only you . . . the one who holds the key to my heart.

Now, tell the truth.
You knew it all along, didn't you?

I love you beary much!